Dedicated to our two legged kids –
Alissa and Seth, and all of our four
legged kids, past and present –
Molly, Roxy, Torii, and Marli.

ISBN 978-0-9829063-2-3
zvvLibrary of Congress Control Number: 2011921437

Torii's Winter Adventure

written by
Janelle Condra

illustrated by
Alan Condra

Hi, my name is Torii.

It is winter here in the woods, which is my favorite place to be in any season. I live where there is lots of snow in the winter. Snow makes playing and exploring so much fun!   Some of my animal friends sleep all winter, but many are out in the woods having fun, too. I go on adventures in the woods in the spring, summer, fall, and even now in the winter! My family comes along, and likes to take pictures of me while I'm on my adventures. They even made me a photo album of my very own so I can share all the fun I've had. I am looking at it right now.

2

3

Come and look at my photo album with me!
You can see how Marli is growing and I will
tell you about my favorite winter holiday —
Christmas! Then I will show you some pictures
of a fun winter adventure in the woods!

Last fall I had a big surprise when my family brought Marli home to live with us. She was little then, but got bigger every day.

We like to play together all the time.
One of our favorite games is tug of war.

6

There are so many fun things about winter. I like playing in the snow, sledding down a big hill, and CHRISTMAS!

Merry Christmas

From Torii

Last year my family made Christmas
cards with a picture of me on the front.

This year Marli and I had a great idea for
our Christmas card. HO! HO! HO!

9

Now Marli is big enough to go with me on my adventures in the woods. There is so much snow here! We have a lot of fun running through the big drifts...

and digging for things buried in the snow.

Look what I found!
I think Marli wants me to share.

Today my family is going to our favorite sledding hill.
Marli and I brought our toboggan. We love riding together
and going fast down the big hill!

Wheee!
Sledding is so much fun!

Wow! That was a wild ride!
"Marli, come over here. I see some tracks.
Maybe we'll find an animal friend who wants to play."

The tracks lead to this hole. I think this is where
Rabbit lives. "Rabbit, are you down there?"

Here's Rabbit, but she is busy eating her lunch.
Maybe she will play with us later.

I hear something inside that cave. Who is
making that noise? I hope they want to play!

Yikes! That sound is Bear snoring! "Come on Marli, we'd better get out of here. Bear will not be happy if we wake him up!"

It is time to go home. We didn't find any animal friends
who had time to play today, but that was a fun winter
adventure in the woods! I hope we can do that again soon!

21

I can't wait to share another fun adventure
with you, but not right now...

it's time for my nap with Marli!

Shhhhhh

Think About the Book
Torii's Winter Adventure
If you don't remember — look back in the book to find the answers!

* What game does Torii like to play with Marli?

* What is Torii's favorite holiday?

* What did Torii find buried in the snow?

* What did Torii and Marli do at the big hill?

* Whose tracks did Torii and Marli find in the snow?

* What did Rabbit have for lunch?

* Who told Torii and Marli not to go in the cave?

* Who was sleeping in the cave?

* What was your favorite part of the book?

Do you remember?

About Torii's Animal Friends

Rabbit

Cottontail rabbits have brown fur, large hind feet, long ears, and a short, fluffy tail that looks like a cotton ball. These rabbits have very good hearing and excellent sight. When they sense danger, they will usually freeze in place unless a predator, such as an owl, coyote, or fox gets too close. Then they will run away quickly, often in a zigzag to confuse their predator. Cottontail rabbits live in many different habitats such as woods, fields, grassy meadows, orchards, and neighborhood yards. Cottontail rabbits are active all year. They usually stay hidden during the day and come out at night to eat. They feed on weeds, grasses, bark, twigs, and crops, such as peas, beans, and lettuce. Babies are born in small ground nests which are lined with fur and grass. Young rabbits grow very fast and are on their own after only three or four weeks!

Cardinal

Northern cardinals, also called redbirds, are easily recognizable songbirds. Males are bright red all over, with a black face around a red bill. Females are light brown with a black face, red bill, and some red on their head, wings, and tail. Both male and female have pointy feathers on top of their heads called a crest. Cardinals can be seen year round, since they do not migrate. They live in backyards, parks, and forest edges and make their nests in shrubs and vines. Pairs mate for life, and stay together through the year. A female will lay three or four pale green eggs with brown spots. The eggs hatch in about 12 days. Predators of cardinals include owls, hawks, snakes, raccoons, and foxes. Cardinals eat mostly fruits and seeds, but will also eat insects, flowers, and buds.

Bear

American black bears have short, round bodies with sturdy legs. Their fur is glossy black except for a tan patch across the nose. Black bears have strong curved claws for climbing trees and soft footpads for moving quietly through the woods. Adult bears can weigh between 120 – 350 pounds. They live in large forested areas with swamps and streams. In early fall black bears stuff themselves with plants, nuts, berries, honey, insects and small mammals. They make dens in hollow trees, brush piles, or caves. In late fall, they hibernate in their dens, feeding on body fat that they have built up. Female black bears give birth to two or three cubs in mid-winter and nurse them in their den until spring. The cubs will stay with their very protective mother for about two years. This picture of a black bear was taken in Torii's own backyard!

About Torii

Torii is a very loyal and loving Golden Retriever. She is friendly to everyone and loves to be petted. Torii was born in the Northwoods of Wisconsin and likes to be outdoors anytime of the year. She loves running through the woods and swimming in the lakes and rivers near her home. In the winter, she has fun playing in the snow.

Whenever Torii goes on an adventure in the woods, she likes to sniff all around and see if she can find any other animals. She would like to be friends with all the forest creatures, but they don't always understand that she just wants to play.

Torii has lots of fun and enjoys living in Wisconsin. If she could really talk, this is what Torii would say –

"Remember life is an adventure – be sure to make it fun!"

Torii's Winter Adventure was illustrated by blending computer graphics backgrounds with actual photographs of Torii going on real life adventures in the woods by her home.

She really does love playing in the snow with Marli!

Meet the Author

Janelle has been a teacher of young children for over 30 years. Living in a small town in northern Wisconsin with her husband Alan has given her the perfect setting to write an adorable book series featuring their golden retriever, Torii. In these creative and amusing books, you can come along on fun adventures with Torii as she explores the woods and visits her animal friends.

Meet the Illustrator

Alan has worked as a professional photographer for over 30 years. He enjoys the outdoors and travels with Torii on her adventures in the woods. Alan has illustrated the book series using some of the many photographs he has taken of Torii, blended with computer graphic backgrounds. This process has created colorful, engaging illustrations that children love!

That was a fun winter adventure! Now join me on spring, summer, and fall adventures by reading the other books in the Torii's Adventures series.

 Happy Reading!

Torii

Torii has fun all year round

Read about her other adventures

Go to toriisadventures.com to learn more

print fun activities about Torii's Adventures!